Resultances

A Breakthrough Book
No. 34

Resultances
Poems by Frank Manley

University of Missouri Press
Columbia & London, 1980

University of Missouri Press, Columbia, Missouri 65211
Library of Congress Catalog Card Number 80–14241
Printed and bound in the United States of America
Copyright © 1980 by Frank Manley

Library of Congress Cataloging in Publication Data

Manley, Frank.
    Resultances: poems.

    (A Breakthrough book; no. 34)
    I. Title.
PS3563.A517R4   811'.54   80–14241
ISBN 0–8262–0312–4

Acknowledgments

Among the poems in this volume, "Retardation Center" was originally
published in *The American Scholar* 46, no. 2 (March 1977); "Faces,"
"Advertisement," and "Lightning Bugs," in *Partisan Review*, copyright ©
1972 by *Partisan Review*; "Giant Swings" in *Partisan Review*, copyright ©
1975 by *Partisan Review*; "Heliogabalus" and "Erasmus in Love" in
Poetry (November 1976); "Unbuilding" in *The Southern Review* 8, no. 4
n.s. (Autumn 1972); "Blackberries" and "Ghost" in *The Southern Review*
10, no. 4 n.s. (Autumn 1974); "Childhood" and "The Spirit of Giving" in
The Southern Review 12, no. 3 n.s. (Summer 1976); and "Going Out" in
Thought 49, no. 193 (June 1974), copyright © 1974 by Fordham
University Press. "Falling" and "Ghost Story" were first published in the
Sewanee Review 82 (1974); "Poor Tom" and "Burning" in the *Sewanee
Review* 84 (1976); and "Gloss" and "Laughter" in the *Sewanee Review* 86
(1978). Copyright © 1974, 1976, 1978 by the University of the South.
Reprinted by permission of the editor. Grateful adcknowledgment is
made to the editors of all these publications for permission to reprint.

For Carolyn

The Devins Award for Poetry

Resultances is the 1980 winner of The Devins Award for Poetry, an annual award originally made possible by the generosity of Dr. and Mrs. Edward A. Devins of Kansas City, Missouri. Dr. Devins was President of the Kansas City Jewish Community Center and a patron of the Center's American Poets Series. Upon the death of Dr. Edward Devins in 1974, his son, Dr. George Devins, acted to continue the Award.

Nomination for the Award is made by the University of Missouri Press from those poetry manuscripts selected by the Press for publication in a given year.

Contents

Whom had that Ancient seen, who thought soules
    made
Of Harmony, he would at next haue said
That Harmony was shee, and thence infer,
That soules were but Resultances from her,
And did from her into our bodies go,
As to our eyes, the formes from obiects flow.

—John Donne

Lightning Bugs

We used to take an old lamp with the bulb out
And a steel wire from a milk-bottle top
Twisted and stuck in the lamp to make contact
And run it out to the hog-wire fence
When they were rising like static around us
And electrocute the lightning bugs in a shower of sparks.
Great power flowed in the current of our hands
As we probed with the electric tip of our minds
For whatever it was in the core of light
That burned all day in the heart of things
And rose in the night, in the dazzling darkness,
And swarmed from the shadowy forms of the earth
Like pulses of thought—the white, elliptical ghosts
Of trees, the fiery tip in each blade
Of grass, and the pastures rising above themselves,
All in their own true forms at last,
Like the souls of the just. And we were plugged into
It all we believed and flowed with a power that leaped
In invisible arcs from the static swirling of stars
In space and the flames of unknown galaxies, down
To our illumined heads and out the sockets
Of our eyes along the wire to the fiery fence,
Where the bugs we impaled turned crisp and died,
Oozing their liquid jelly of light
While we turned green as fox fire, our hands
And mysterious fingers, even the hair and grain of our skin
Streaked and smeared with gleams of solid light.
And then, then we stalked through the dark of our
    childhood
Like *ignes fatui* following the luminous forms
Of ourselves, grim as ghosts haunting our bodies
Back to the blinding effulgence of home.

Heliogabalus

When the Emperor Heliogabalus
Was told by a Syrian oracle
That he would die a violent death,
He had a special noose prepared
Of woven blue and scarlet silk
And a Nubian slave to carry it by day
And sleep with it by his side at night
So that he could be garroted in imperial purple
By his own shadow.
And he had golden swords prepared,
Poisons from Egypt, conclusions infinite
Of easy ways to die
Coiled in the cunning hollow of a ring—
Carnelians, sapphires, emeralds, diamonds,
Carbuncles rounder than a woman's breast
Contrived to suck the blood asleep—
And in the courtyard built a tower
Higher than the topmost turrets of Rome,
The swirling grain of the scaffolding
Gilded in patterns of solid gold,
Steps inlaid with precious stone,
Jade and lapis lazuli,
And there he would run when death
Came after and fling himself off
So that all men forever would be struck dumb
At the wonder and the beauty and the glory of his going—
The elegance and mastery of Heliogabalus,
The last of the line of the Antononies.

But when the time came for his death
And Fate led the Praetorian Guard
To attack the palace and free the state,

They found the Emperor coiled like a snake
Inside the cunning hollow of a privy.
When he was killed, he fell in the pit.
They dug him out and lashed him to an axle
And dragged him through the squares of the city,
Through the dust of the track at the Circus.
Then they stuffed him in a sewer,
But he got stuck halfway in,
And they weighted him with stones instead
And threw him off the Aemilian Bridge
So no one could ever bury the body.
The soldiers who killed him spoke no Latin.
The Senate ordered his name erased
From public works and public record.
But the people remembered. They called him
Big Ass and Shit Face
And told the story from father to son
While the story held up.
And then they forgot him.

Except for some. They are the ones
Who are haunted in sleep by a freckled hand
That holds a severed head like a lantern
And a voice that says over and over:
                The time is free.

Faces

When the XIX Legion was caught in the swamps of the
    Rhine
And bushwacked there by the natives,
Their armor dragging them into the mud,
And not a man among them lived to tell how they died
Or what they caught in the frame of their face
When the last stroke fell,
And when Germanicus found them at last,
They were gone.
The mud had grown over the ripples they made.
Only their faces, nailed to the trees, remained.

When Jezebel, the haughty queen of an alien land,
Ran barefoot through all the men in her court,
Touching their hearts lightly
With the crescent of her toes, the palms of her hands
Easing their flesh as she ran,
They gave her to the dogs at last
In the heat of her running, the burst of her lungs,
And they pulled her down, and they ate her
Except for the soles of her lovely feet
And the white palms of her hands.

Erasmus in Love

Cras amet qui nunquam amavit quique amavit
Cras amet, Erasmus wrote. And then he reflected.
That girl across the room beside the stove,
That girl, he wrote, is in my head.
Those breasts I see are bulging in the sockets of my eyes.
This table too is in my head.
He reflected the table like the girl reflected the heat
Of the stove. These walls, these other people—
All in my head. She smiled, he wrote, smiling.
And now she's talking. Now she turns. Her rump
Slides on the chair, flattened out on each side,
Bulging. She leans forward. Her breasts dazzle
My eyes. The light falls from the air.

It's cold over here away from the stove, Erasmus
Wrote. The stove stinks like bacon grease.
Red with rust like raw skin. The people
Stink like the stove. The ice in the river freezes
In my veins. Who is that she's talking to?
Erasmus wrote. Why does she smile at him?
If this is all in my head, she ought
To smile at me, he reflected. Everyone
Else in the room—the farmers, the merchants, the
    travelers—
All leave to go to the bathroom at once.
Winter blasts in. We are suddenly alone.
She rocks her chair forward at me, leg
Tipping leg, and I reflect her coming,
He wrote, unbottoning her blouse. Her breasts
Swing free. She touches the nipple, smiling
At me. I am reflecting like a stove.
Winter blasts the room again. The people
Rush in. And she's back in her place at the stove.

Why does that always happen to me? Erasmus
Wrote. Why does everyone always come back
From the bathroom? Why do I always reflect things
Like that? he reflected. I should have said,
Here, let me help you, or, Hello, I am Erasmus.
Who are you, inching your chair over at me,
Touching your nipples, spreading your legs? But how
Was I to know it wasn't in my head
When everything else I see is there—this table,
These people, who never go to the bathroom anymore?
And whose head am I in? Erasmus wrote,
And why do you always do this to me?
Why do you send her here, and others like her,
Wherever I go? They ride up on mules, sleek
And naked as the flanks of beasts. Eyes like cows.
Udders like goats. They make obscene gestures in upstairs
Windows, come out of dark woods, behind
Trees, around corners. They come at me
In my sleep and always walk past me, Erasmus
Wrote, because I suspect they are in my head.

All of a sudden he put down the pen and stared
Across the room at me. I tried to look busy,
The checkers suddenly complicated as chess. I started
To talk to the girl again, asked her her name.
She shifted her hips and squirmed a little. Erasmus
Still stared. So I figured, what the hell.
I took her by the hand and led her over.
I leaned forward. His breath smelled like fish.
I said, are you the illustrious Desiderius Erasmus
Of Rotterdam, Light of the North? Yes, indeed, he said,
I am. Fingers twitching. I said, let me
Introduce to you Marilyn de Kooning. Delighted,
He murmured. I have often admired you from afar.

The breasts you point I have cupped in my hands.
The hands you hold in your lap like pigeons,
I have seen above my head making signs
From top-story windows. Your eyes have ridden
Before me over the Alps. I dreamed of you once
In More's garden, and at banquets of kings and great
Princes, you were under the table at work.
Excuse me a moment, Erasmus said, and he picked
Up the pen. His eyes turned inward.
He started to fade, like light after sunset.
She stands up, Erasmus wrote, swings
A shawl around her head. Skin translucent
As the stove. She walks across the room.
Her ass shimmers like heat, and I am reflecting.

Years later, in the portrait by Dürer, his skin
Pouchy as unbaked bread, arthritic fingers
Like tendrils twisted beside a bowl of flowers,
Erasmus wrote a gloss on a love poem,
Explaining that it is all in your head.
Love will come in a rushing of wind, he wrote.
Lust will leap in your veins like a goat over
A fence, and you will see her, Erasmus wrote,
Naked as the sky in the summer. She will shimmer like heat
Coming toward you and say, Erasmus, Erasmus mine,
I waited for you beside the great oaks
On the roadway I heard you would pass.
I lingered at wells while my parents called in the dark.
I saw you from my bedroom window, with my husband
Asleep on the bed beside me. I waved at you
And showed you my name, gave you a sign of my love.
I have dipped my handkerchief in my own blood
And wiped your saddle, cut my hair and bound it
To the tail of your horse to draw you to me.

I sat across from you in the stove rooms
Of innumerable inns while you wrote and looked
But did not see. And now you are mine
Erasmus wrote. We will love here forever.

This was in Washington, in the National Gallery.
I saw the wild flowers, the aged desperate
Face and took out a piece of paper
And began to write. He took off his clothes, I wrote,
His cassock, his ermine, even the hard-earned stones
On his fingers. He laid them neatly in a pile
And walked toward her, shaking the wrinkles loose
As he went, shedding his skin like smoke in the winter.
She shimmered before him like sunlight on fast-moving
    water.
When the guard got to me, I had her dress
Halfway up her hip. A scream panicked
Inside her throat like the sounds of hoofs in a pen,
and I thought, Erasmus, you old bastard you.

Falling

The calls I dread come every night
As soon as I've fallen inside myself

Before I hit bottom and die
In my sleep. My father's weary voice
Comes through the burning core in the heart

Of the wire. He calls me to tell of his falling:
A toy on a string in my hand.

His voice is almost too high to be heard.
It hums on the wire inside my head,
The sound of my blood, the same thing

Over and over, like a busy signal:
First death, first death.

Advertisement

I wonder whatever happened to
The beautiful advertisements of my youth
I used to see through the bars of the streetcar windows
Lurching to town in the old inevitable way
Where everything I knew I loved and loved because I knew
Slid through my heart like blood on iron wheels,
The cleanest dreams in town . . .

I mean the mysterious things in the billboards
That said, Just like mother made,
Only more so. Things you couldn't understand.
Or the 100-year-old bread
(Long corridors and dusky limbs of Egyptian
Girls, dancing at orgies. A sudden plague.
Immediate death. And the bread on the table
Uneaten. Unearthed a hundred years later
By sterilized men in beards and white coats
Who carry it in wrappers of antique gold
To the A&P across the park for the Keenans),
Or the Planters Peanut that walked the streets and gave
Himself away on a spoon, with the imploring eyes
Of a man inside the uncracked shell of death,
Or the car in the tree forty feet high
(Amos' Auto Parts and Welding Service)
And me wondering how it got there
Through most of the days of my formative years
And learning at last in the stillness of sleep that it grew
There, the rusting petals of the yellow convertible
Clashing like thunder at night in its angry unfolding.

All the innocent, contrived conceits of my boyhood,

Polished and mannered as my grandfather, who lived
By a code of ethics in business and died, in a way,
Like a man who stuck his humming head inside
The engine of a car at Hendrick's Service Station
And had it eaten off up to the hips,
The legs still there when I was a boy,
Dribbled on the edge of the open maw like seaweed,
Sucking in the customers rain or shine.

Burning

Fulgebunt iusti, et tanquam scintillae in arudineto discurrent.

—Sapientia 3:7

We knocked them out with a two-by-four
All summer long it seemed,
Crouching like gargoyles on the rafters
Or Russian dancers stored in a squat.
We swarmed like wasps in a nest on fire
And punched great jagged holes at the sky
With the blunting ends of our wooden arms,
And the old boards, the shingles,
Flew up, out, and fell,
The unexpected attic open to the sky
For once and once only—
Old rags, old mason jars,
Grease from old fires, old squirrel
Nuts, wasp nests, and us,
Breaking our way out, piecing the sky
Together, punch by ragged punch.

And after the new roof was on,
The tin in the morning gray as deep water,
Shining with oil in the light,
The shingles surrounded the house like a ring
Of fire one hundred years old.
And we hauled them wheelbarrow by wheelbarrow
Full for the rest of the long summer
It seemed, down by the fallen barn,
Dropping them off like dinosaur tailings,
The tunnels of some giant mole.

And then she comes and sorts them out.
In an overgrown lot by a fallen barn,
With a forest of windblown timber around her,
The slash of the great oaks lying
In tangles, she squats and orders the shingles,
Slow as rocks on a building wall.
She stacks them like dishes or slices of bread
And carries them back, arms full of fire . . .
While halfway up the hill behind the house,
The chain saw roaring in my head,
The windblown oaks falling around in my buzzing,
I get to what I think is work.
But when I haul the logs back home
And split them with wedges of cold in the yard,
The kitchen is already roaring darkly in the corner,
And the open hole in the living room wall
Is boarded up with sheets of solid flame.

And suddenly the sky is punched out of my head
And something inside me swarms
As I see her sit in the flames,
The hair of her glowing head transparent
As smoke, bones burning inside her skin
Like shadows in coals. She catches in sunlight.
Her flesh shines. She burns in my mind
Like sparks in a field of dry grass.

Retardation Center

There in that place where each one is different,
Strange as God made us, the blind and the deaf
Grope at the world, or hang in a hug forever.
Smiles and tears are ready as feet to run.
Floors and walls are there to bounce off,
And demons appear in the middle of day.
There are minds so deep, so sunk
In their bodies, the flesh folds over
And ingrows itself to a sort of laugh
Feeling food, its texture and smell.
This is the place where those end up
Who were born with their souls for a body.
They are what they are.

Here

It is too good
at night after work when I go home
to those I feel I am at last
beginning truly to love

and hear the voices playing in the yard
like my own best thoughts
in the air-conditioned sunroom
with the great world somewhere

in the roaring of the traffic
beyond the childish singing of my soul
and peace at last is with me in the room
familiar as the stranger in the mirror.

It is too good after my wife
has finished all the days of her life
to see at last a flash of light
across her eyes a moment in the west

and sit and think each one alone
of the evening in comfort before us
and what we can do with the rest of our lives
after all our loves and all our denials.

For they are too good
and there is nothing we can do
except to make them more
like images of images

reflections of reflections in the mirror.
And after the evening has wasted
and we fall in our familiar bed
we dream of the roaring of traffic

of hard driving through country
of hand-lettered signs on rocks in the mountains
and the madmen who made them
who cry like wind and tell us

we will meet God face to face
like mirrors in the mirrors of his eyes
who tell us we will never wake
and never sleep again.

And when we wake we know
that all of this is good.
This is my place my father's house
and his father's before him.

There is nothing here I do not love
and did not work all my life to get
and all of this is mine.
All of this is mine

except for the rushing of wind in my sleep
like fire the distant roaring
of blood a clouded mirror
and the face that suddenly appears.

On First Looking into Girls

We always knew, like stout Cortez.
We always knew from the way they walked.
Girls who were putting out regular
moved in the hips like a locomotive.
The body remembered, we figured,
or maybe it got permanently dislocated,
the pelvis popped, froze open from screwing.
We studied for weeks that pure serene
like forelorn watchers of the sky
when a new planet swims into their ken,
staring so hard we finally saw
or imagined we saw in X-ray vision
the one eye under the skirt
open the wrinkles of its lid
and stare back at us in wild surmise.

In Praise of Folly

When Erasmus went backwards over the Alps,
Riding his sciatica like an elephant, he heard
The ghost of Livy whisper in his ear:
You will freeze in the passes, cut the rocks with fire
And vinegar, eat strange flesh, and drink
The gilded stale of puddles. The snow will lie
Hard on the rocks. The air will thin, trees
Disappear. Elephants will lose their footing.
Struggling to get up, they will lie
On their sides like beetles. Livy said:
You will endure all this, the perils of conquest,
Because you are chosen, out of Africa,
The smell of the Orient still in your hair.
Erasmus shifted his weight on the mule, easing
His hip, and thought of the swaying rump,
The fragile basket riding the broad back,
Reeds from Chad, the distant Niger, the Nile,
And thought of an army behind him marching upward
Out of Italy, struggling over the rocks
Of the goat path, feet wrapped in rags,
The edges of spears glinting in sunlight,
And turned his good ear to the wind to catch
The words at the top of the pass. Livy said:
After the last peak, the plains of Europe
Will lie before you: The land of promission, flowing
With fat, with corn and honey, straw-haired
Women and idle men with bodies like women.
Yoke them, my son, and plow the state.
And Erasmus thought of the books he would write,
The conquests, the riches possessed. He thought of the earth
And all its kingdoms and the glory of them lying

Before him, after the long march, and the anguish was on
   him.
His hard eyes narrowed like matches, gazing upward
As in a vision at the same cliffs Lowell
Would later see from his berth on the Paris express.
"Each backward wasted Alp," he wrote, "a Parthenon,"
"Fire-branded socket of the cyclop's eye,"
And then went on to muse about Hellas and the lack
Of tickets to that altitude. But Erasmus saw
The sun on the peaks like his own best thoughts
And lumbered on without a guide, leading
His army into the defiles, into the sheer
Cliffs of fall, into the snowfields and blinding light
While Livy whispered: Hannibal failed. Hannibal
Went backwards over the Alps with hardly
An elephant left. But you, my son, will rise
Like the coming of light in the east. You will prevail
Over darkness. And Erasmus listened, for Erasmus believed
What Livy said. Believed it was perfect history.

Terminus

One side is bright
The other is dark
The grass is silver
The flowers explode
We walk in the garden
He stands like a shaft
His eyes are stone
They look at the sun
We cannot see
What he holds in his hand
Only above us
The moon rising

Childhood

When I was a boy and visited Scranton,
Where I was born but never grew up,
The first thing I did
Was go down the mines

To see where I came from.
The thing I remember were empty corrals
Where they kept the mules to haul
The roaring cars through the tunnels.

Bred underground, in the dazzling darkness,
The coals of their eyes had burned to ash.
The sockets were all white.
They moved along guided by tracks.

My grandfather when he was a boy
Started to work when he was seven
Picking slate three stories up
In the windless tunnel of the roaring chute.

The thing I loved was a child like me:
The shaft of his mind a dazzling darkness.
His thoughts were all white.
His hands moved guided by tracks.

Dead Letters

The safety deposit box
Had a hole in it
Plugged up
With a note that said
There wasn't anything here in the first place

And that was it
Except for some used furniture
Only a drunk would haul away
Or St. Vincent de Paul's
Or a drunk working for St. Vincent de Paul's

I cleaned out the apartment
Had the mail forwarded
The unpaid last few months of his life
And then one night on the parapet—

No.
That's not right.
That was later.

The first letter I got from my father
After he died
Was from New Guinea
It said
The natives are starving Frank
Waiting for parachutes
Send five dollars
Quick

A week later from Guatemala
The letter said
This is no vacation Frank
I am in the mountains
With Camilo Torres
We have bombed the President's Palace
We sleep in ancient ruins
And wait for government trucks to pass
Send five dollars in care of the Melvilles

In Cuba
In Cuernavaca with Ivan Illich
In Baltimore at Jonah House
My father was there
Shuffling to Selma
Paying bond
Hustling votes in Mississippi
Getting killed and buried under a dam
Walking down a road alone
Tar hot under his feet
The do-rag tied in knots on his head
Waiting for the sniper

While ten nuns in Savannah Georgia
Discalced Carmelites eighty years old
Were praying in shifts
Perpetually
Twenty-four hours a day
For the repose of his soul
My father among them scribbling furiously

Send more money Frank
Wire it collect
Write a check on the back of this holy picture
On the calendar
Count the days of your life
The poor are bleeding to death
The poor are starving Frank
The poor are in jail with no one to help them
The children are dying Frank
They are brain damaged

They are burned to death in frying pans
By parents
Who were burned to death in frying pans
They are beaten by fathers
Who can't find work
While all the cars in the world
Creep up on New York City
The cars are brain damaged Frank
Send five dollars

Quick
Here's a scapular
Three hundred and sixty-five Masses a year
Visits to the Blessed Sacrament
Novenas   litanies
Thirty years plenary indulgence

In every letter to the dead
From every otherworldly
Catholic charity
He ever sent five dollars to
My father's restless spirit
Roams the world
Crying
List list oh list

Like the other night on the parapet
Rumors of invasion
A blood-red moon
Carousing in the palace
Far below
Silence   darkness
And there beyond the battlements
The very shape and gesture of his thought
He spoke to me in his native tongue

I could a tale unfold
He said
Whose lightest word
Would harrow up thy soul
Freeze thy young blood
Make thy two eyes
Like stars
To start from their spheres
Thy knotted and combined locks to part
And each particular hair
To stand on end
Like quills upon the fretful porcupine
But this eternal blazon must not be
To ears of flesh and blood
List list oh list
If ever thou didst thy dear father love
Send five dollars

And I said
In the same language
Rest, rest, perturbéd spirit
But I thought to myself
Oh cursed spite that ever I was born to set it right
And then I thought

Nay

Come

Let's go together

Laughter

You have a sudden laugh, a way of throwing
Back your head and tearing loose from me
That breaks my heart to see you so abandoned
And alone in your delight: innocent as a child
Playing with herself, sluttish, lost in happiness;
No longer lonely and never more alone.

I stand outside the window and watch you
Naked, key cold in my desire
To turn the lock and slip into your laughter,
Riding the crest until I overtake you
And both burst through to one another,
Coupled in the undertow like sharks. Ourselves.

The Spirit of Giving

My grandfather on my mother's side
Once got a present for Christmas at work
Banded with steel and riveted shut
Like a payroll box for a million dollars
That bounced off a stagecoach, ran over
Three horses, two dogs, and a cactus,
Hit a boulder and went right on through.
It was painted all over: DONT OPEN
TILL XMAS. That was October.

Under the tree with sleep in his eyes,
Needles falling all over like dandruff,
Kids of all sizes under his skin,
An ostrich in a nest of bright tinsel
Stolen from Bedouin asleep in oases,
The dreams of eight children open around him,
He brooded like the last king of Tara,
The ruins of his glory shrunk to one box,
And labored all morning through all the Masses,
Miraculous births, and the spirit of giving
Till late afternoon he pried up the lid
And out ran a million bits of bright things,
Crawling and creeping like thoughts sprouted legs—
Ants, maybe, or roaches, baby crickets,
Midges and gnats—some kind of bugs
Visible only to magnified eyes,
Blowing up like a sandstorm at dawn:
Under the sofa, up on the table,
Swarmed up the tree and buzzed at the lights,
Swung from the tinsel, swooped down on the manger

Like hordes of Bedouin after the Magi
For stealing their camels and tinsel for gifts,
Climbed in with the baby, tumbled the bedclothes,
Rummaged the straw and the ass of the ass.
Stealthy as lice, they burrowed in dolls' hair
And ran up their dresses quick as a hand.
My grandmother had what she called a mild seizure,
Mostly to do with her stockings and legs.
The children quit eating. Creation was crawling.
God's plenty was moving like on the Sixth Day.
My grandfather—stunned as Adam first waking—
Opened his eyes to a world of new light.
The spirit of giving took over the house.

Ghost

for Ben Mathis

In every nail sunk into every board,
In every sill still levered there,
The muscles of my back still hold it up.
And my hands shape the waters that still fall
From the molded pine of the trough at the spring.
My mind turned on the lights,
Like tendons ran the wires where the current flows,
Cut the glass and placed the windowpanes,
Sharp as pain in the light.
And when I walk the whole damn house is mine.

And sometimes at noon in the valley,
In the grass cut over and over in the sunlight,
In the hefted shapes of the stones of the terraces,
Heavy as my own body to lift, I am seen—
In the dirty knuckles and fists of the roots,
Where I lay forgotten till I came back
And grew in the arms of the muscadine,
Twisted and clenched from the neck on down.
Look at these swollen, bloody fists.
This whole damn place here is mine.

Going Out

Outside the house
year after year
the rot inside each drop of rain
inside the friction of the wind
the smell of a cellar
the color of lichens on stone
the light coming through
from inside the boards
like light in a wasp nest
and the house going back
inside the storm
inside the tearing
the grinding of tin

Inside the house
something had happened
something got loose and stayed inside
in the hole of the chimney
something was there
the walls ripped and hanging in sheets
the pile of dirty clothes in the corner
something had torn it with knives
and was there
in the shattered glass on the floor
sharp as hate

And on the wall
a sign
like a suicide note
saying

WE GOING OUT
AND ETERNATY
TO MEET GOD

RU READY
GODS CLOCK IS TICKING
AWAY ITS TIME

saying o yes
we all going out
after the murder
after the last knife of the looting
the rape of the old clothes of our body
we going out
for god's clock is ticking
inside the rain
scratching the wasp nest wall of our skull
god's clock is ticking
inside the wind of our lives
inside the wind of our breath
god's clock is ticking
inside the storms
that sweep around us at night
with the screeching of tin
that rips at the top of our skull
god's clock is ticking
inside the shine of our bones
burning inside us
and we going out
o yes we going out
we all going out of that house

Origin of the Species

Dogs are all doomed.
They cannot survive.
They screw your guests
Below the knees
And hump the furniture.
They shit in the streets
And piss on small children.
Sometimes they eat them.
They also eat garbage.
Dogs have bad breath.
Their eyes are sad.
They sleep in the sun
And need to be consoled.

Dogs are like dinosaurs.
The last ones are shrinking.
They never go out.
They sit in your lap
And smell good.
They have no fleas,
Nothing to bark at.
They turn into cats.

And the cats will survive.
They shit in boxes
And cover it up.
They are always alone.
Cats are like grease.
They make no noise.
They care about nothing.
Cats stay in houses
And never get lost.
They look out of windows.
They are always thinking.
Cats are like people.
Cats will inherit the earth.

Fig Bush

Master, look! The fig bush you cursed is dried up

—Mark 11:21

Beside the light wood of the wall
Where the sun sat under the leaves
Like an old man in a Victorian garden,
I planted the fig bush,
Exotic as Priapus this far north,
And waited for the fruit to swell like testicles.

And every winter the fig bush I planted
Withered from my thirtieth year,
Thin as the bones of a paralyzed man
With a devil in him,
Touched by the weather
And died to the ground.

And every spring it started again,
The sparse, thin growth of the risen plant
Spreading like lust,
The strange leaves unfolding,
But bore no fruit.
Surely it's cursed.

The cold air dazzles.
The years inside me unfold.

Blackberries

When they're in at the cove as long as my thumb,
I say to my knuckle-faced fist full of neighbors,
Like a hound that's been beaten a little too hard,
"A smart man hadn't got sense how to grow them."

They smile like splits in a piece of pine.

But they come. They put down the fields
That harrow them clean of briars and weeds,
They cut loose the tractors to run with the dogs,
And they come and stand around for a while
With nothing to do and no way to do it.
They grow into ease like an empty field,
In patches of talk, with buckets and hip boots
And long hungry bellies for what you can't
Grow and can't hardly chew up and swallow—
For pinecones and briars and knotweeds and rocks,
Whatever tastes wild and goes down hard.

We drink at the spring and talk about snakes.

Above the spring the cove lies low,
Still as a snake in its coil of land.
We wade in the canes till they're over our heads,
And one by one they swallow us whole
Till no one is left but each one alone,
Chained to the spot of our mortal flesh

By the sinewy whiplash we stir up around us
And eating as fast as our hands can move,

Full of the taste of hard-bitten things.

We sweat in the stillness and bleed on the quiet,
Filling like summer and almost as slow,
Till one by one we explode into walking
And startle ourselves to come back again.
We gather together like parts of a body
Fresh risen, uncertain of where they fit in,
And drink us some whiskey to settle our brains.
We talk about hunting and fishing and women
And what we have gotten and what we can't get.

The whippoorwills finally use up the daylight.

At home in the lamplight the berries flash dark
In the well of the buckets like droppings of day.
In the sweat of the kitchens the women prepare them
And render them harmless as good as they can
With sacksful of sugar and thick crusts of pastry
That pop your teeth open, sprouting with seeds,
While out in the parlors the men drink more whiskey
And stare at the windows that stare back at them.
They wash off the rank smell they carry
Inside them and sleep with their women,
A tangle of still canes that gleam in the moonlight,

Dreaming of nothing, gone wild again.

Louis II

Louis II of Hungary who drowned in a bubble of earth by
the Danube was said to have been born with no skin on his
body he glistened like a pearl and when the wind blew his
muscles shuddered like leaves on a tree the sunlight was
unendurable and the full moon inflamed him women were
attracted to him they could look into his arm forever the
twist of his thigh the tendons and sinews of his hand strok-
ing the while their own blind breasts in bed they could
watch the pleasure building and not only feel but see the
body's excitement when they stroked his flesh it ran under
their hands like grass he fired and flamed his bones like
shadows and when he rode in his armor to fight the Turks
they oiled him and slid him in the metal casing closing
around him like skin the steel was cold the sides of his ribs
burned against the sides of the metal and after a day of hard
fighting he lay in the river like a swaying weed the water
flowing through him like fingers sliding in beneath his ribs
and touching him down to the dim quick of his soul and he
was sensitive to people their shadows falling on him caused
him pleasure and pain and at Buda when he rode through
the streets the press of his subjects the breath of the mob
cheering and shouting came over him like bird wings beat-
ing when he died at Mohacs escaping the Turks the skin of
the earth rose up before him swelled in a bubble and burst

46

New Colt

Whatever it is is coming through
the darkness of our eyes
to deliver us of the steps
and the dream of the chain
and the tractor straining
the colt pulled free at last
through light as thick
as the grain of a cloth
to the shotgun tunnel of still dark
the abandoned broiler house
aimed at our heads.

And there it is new made
the first awakened nightmare
in our lives stepped free
and coming toward us
steady as the finger on a trigger moving
coming on incongruous as death
like a shot that bursts
through the pupils of our eyes
and just stands there
total as sunlight
indifferent as a wild dog.

Feet

Feet are like souls, they never wear out,
They carry the shape and heft of the body,
And like us they rest at night

Folded like hands, gripping each other
Or sticking out from under the covers.

And like us, they dream. Feet dream
Each night of how it will be
When all their burdens are lifted

And they go on air or hang down
Under our wings like the feet of birds.

Feet dream of resurrected feet,
Fresh risen from water, rosy
With steam, pink and shining with light.

First Eclogue

When I was a boy, lean and tough as thought,
The dogs were still at Emory, and I would
Read in the marble library all day
Till the grass and the trees and the sky were changed
And burst with light in the slanting sun, each
Pine top spiked with gold, each leaf transparent.
Or I would sing in my carrel all summer
While the dogs slept on in the shadowed grass.
Pleased with the shade in the marble cool world
I slept like the dogs who slept like God—my wife
Young and beautiful and the dogs sleeping under
The trees, in the halls, or on the worn marble stairs.
They slept through all my years at school,
A changing pack of hounds and feists, setters
And beagles, groaning and stretching and farting in quiet,
Each in his solitude, while overhead
Ancient voices moved through waves of heat:
Nos patriae fines, et dulcia linquimus arva;
Nos patriam fugimus.

Gloss

"Onely death addes t'our length,"
John Donne says, crazy as ever,

When all day long my wife can tuck
Her tricky head beneath my chin

And in our bed at night,
Eyes on a level with mine,

Toes frozen to touching toes,
She adds to my length and grows,

As we tuck each other
One another in.

Wilderness

On 5 May 1864
When Abner Small went out to look for men who had run
The darkness he moved in was visible

Humps of honeysuckle
Hung from the trees like sharpshooters
The underbrush huddled like lines of skirmishers
And everywhere the fires
The wounded crept about like flames
And the animals were gone
And only the night remained there
Only the smoke like the smell of darkness
Whole pine trees burned like candles

When Abner Small went out into the Wilderness
Looking for men on their feet still running
He saw a shell burst overhead
Like a great comet or bolt of lightning
The darkness lifted
And he saw before him the trees appear
Each vine each leaf each blade of grass
Distinct in the overwhelming light
He startled at the sudden glare
And kicked up the smoldering flames in the leafmold
A shower of sparks flew out from his feet
Like footsteps his spirit took
Like the footprints of his soul before him

And he saw a man with red hair and beard
He lay like a pile of dead leaves
A mound of briars or honeysuckle
The flames reached him
They lit in his beard and his beard burned
His red hair flamed
And the cartridges at his belt exploded
And Abner Small saw in the new light
Who the man looked like
His beard and red hair
He saw his own side explode
And his own eyes stare at himself
And discovered the man he was sent for

And in the quick light of the shell
He saw a white dogwood in bloom
The pale flowers red in the firelight
He saw the whole tree blossom at once
Leaf bole fuse and flower
In one blinding moment of light
Like the petals of the soul
Burning inside him
As the flames licked the tips of his eyes
And the glowing coals touched his lips
He heard a voice from the burning bush
Like the sound of his breath
Inward and outward
Saying forever
I am who am
I am who am

Giant Swings

Cette pensée, ce perfectionnement matériel, cette harmonie, cette
    nuance particulière d'amour, . . . je ne puis croire que, dans
    leur chair, ils mourront completement.

—Pierre Teilhard de Chardin

The whole thing has a ring of granite,
a wall of granite around it like a magic circle
now, holding in the gray sides of my head,
the eroding sand and the clay where the grass never
grew, under the high-pruned magnolias,
the water oaks . . . And there it is summer.
The streetlights come on and boys still
gather thick as bugs and sing in the dark
like whippoorwills the same song over and over
in circles, going inside and outside themselves—
hanging in air like fish in the water
performing whatever crazy things our bodies
tell us to, eyes popping with the strain,
muscles twisted like rope, and the world sluing
around and around the bar in a giant swing—
going into a kick, a sharp jerk down,
then rising in flight on something inside us
that jumps through our skin and carries us with it
and us holding on, the bar climbing in front of us,
our murderous bodies going on past
and then going over and out as we gain
our momentum and break the surface like flying fish.
The taps on the heels and toes of our shoes flash
in the darkness. The lights in the windows of houses
we see as we fly, the neon signs of the drugstore
all in a blur as we go in circles like planets
arcing the sky, like pinwheels of flesh,

kicking up sparks from our flashing heels
and move with a motion not wholly our own
till the stars that swim in the blood of our eyes
turn into the lights of the park, turn into
the windows of all the houses to come in our lives
and all the people inside them we love.
And only the bar was real. The bar led
us up and slowly lowered us down
as the giant swing lost its momentum
and we swung in staggering arcs and dropped off
and fell like death in a pile of bones on the sand,
then rose again, stunned into life, forever inside the wall.

Ghost Story

They asked for it, safe in their flannel cocoons
For the night, prepared to sleep and dream
Into their chrysalis of day.

So I told them of Tickanately Church,
That sits high on the flashing river,
Washed with the blood of its burying ground,
And how its lonely bell would ring
That very night, when long nails
Scratched at the pine of the coffin
Till clod by clod the grave unburied itself
And the shapeless thing took shape again,
Rising to scatter the plastic flowers
And all the names turned into stone at Tickanately Church,
Slashing the ground with its long nails
In the immortal, mysterious hate of the dead.

And suddenly I scared myself.
I saw myself in the lonely clay of Tickanately Church,
Tearing the flowers my children brought
On sunlit days in the upper air,
While close in the night,
In the house made tight with the strength of my arms,
My children slept into age.

Unbuilding

All summer long the apples fell
on the bleeding tin of the roof
and exploded up the valley like a shot
that stopped the summer dead
like a damn fool hunter
from Atlanta gotten loose,
mired to his ass in the blackberry canes,
firing distress in the head
high weeds of the abandoned fields,
or tripped on his rifle and died out of season.

And buried myself in the stomped-out place,
mired in a slashing of blackberry canes,
usually at work unbuilding the barn,
I'd pause, the hammer misfired in my hand,
and listen for whatever it was
got loose, for the sound of hammers
more distant, echoes but never the same,
unbuilding   unbuilding.

In winter now the roof is gone.
The ax-squared rafters frame the sky,
and the apples fall in their season,
catch for a time where the roof should be
and go on through in silence.
And the deer came down from the mountains at night
crossing the flattened fields in silence,
utterly beyond themselves, gigantic
in the moonlight. They pause in silence at the frame,
in silence go on through and gorge themselves.

Poor Tom

I can understand the monkeys, Thomas,
And a weasel or two, some parrots in cages,
Maybe even a Barbary ape, a gift
From the Spanish ambassador for services rendered.
Good for the children. Part of the plan.
Not that Erasmus would ever approve.
St. Jerome's lion was more his style:
In a desert, where the sun bears down
As sharp as his mind without shadow.
Your beasts, Thomas, were caged in a garden,
Shaded by shrubs, behind the house.
Henry Patenson fed them, a natural,
Grinning and smacking his lips as they ate.
Dame Alice could hardly tell you apart.
And sometimes on Fridays—I understand, Thomas—
Leaving the shape of your life at the altar,
The heretics bound and lashed in your study,
You'd visit in private the king and his council,
The great lords at Lambeth, in cages,
God's creatures all—antic, amusing:
Weasel or monkey or parrot or ape.
You could hardly tell them apart,
You, the only free man among them.
I understand that. Hall said you joked
Your way to the scaffold: a matter of style.

But Cliff, Thomas—Cliff. What cage
Or cell did you keep him in
After you took him by the hand
And led him away from knocking the heads
Off statues of saints on the bridge to the Tower?
Where did he stay in the garden?
And what did you see in him, Thomas?

Compassion, perhaps, a work of mercy?
Or did you see yourself there at last?
The mad eyes innocent and full of anger,
Caged in himself: your own *momento mori,*
The head and the sharpened ax the same:
The outcast, the shape of your life at the altar?
Cliff waits in the cage, Thomas.
He cannot rest. He cannot be kept,
Cannot be loosed till the king claims
The garden and the cages all open.
Then Cliff roams free,
And your head returns to its place on the bridge.
Your distant eyes look down from the pike.
They do not see Cliff pass in the crowd.
He walks on the water, over the Thames,
Other things on his mind now,
Not heads, looking for something
To find in a storm, somewhere to rest,
Some hovel. Poor Tom,
Poor Turleygod, poor Tom.

Plato's Cave:
Chicken Little and the Holy Ghost

Inside the dark tunnel
where someone before me
grew chickens like crops
in the light of eternal day
I brood on the grainy ladders
of sun where the roof
has collapsed into glory
and wait for the sky to fall.
My feet in the dung of the ages
I hear the whir of the ghostly
wings the fiery cackle
of tongues in the dark
and hatch myself into silence.

Resultances

Poems by
Frank Manley

The poems in *Resultances* were written from 1972 to 1977. Most of them are inextricably bound up in history—personal history and public history, the history of the individual and the history of the history of race. They are poems of archetypical experience—childhood, sex, adolescence, the death of parents, and the experience of love. Manley draws on his knowledge of history and literature for inspiration in his poems. His imagination allows him to depict Desiderius Erasmus, Abner Small, and Louis II of Hungary as they never were, and to write of Heliogabalus, St. Thomas More, and Ben Mathis as they might have been. The title of the collection is from a line in Donne's *Anniversaries*: "That Harmony was shee, and thence infer, / That soules were but Resultances from her."

Winner of the 1980 Devins Award for Poetry, **Frank Manley** is Professor of English at Emory University. He is the author of numerous articles and poems, as well as the editor of several books including John Donne's *The Anniversaries* (The Johns Hopkins University Press, 1963) and Sir Thomas More's *A Dialogue of Comfort Against Tribulation* (Yale University Press, 1977).

ISBN 0−8262−0312−4 $10.00

A Breakthrough Book No. 34

University of Missouri Press
P.O. Box 1644   Columbia, Missouri 65205